World One Currency Manifesto

By Dr. Michelle Augustine

Also by Dr. Michelle Augustine

THE TRADER*
PABLO, A COYOTE STORY

In production:

FINANCIAL CRASH
WOMAN OF (SERIES)
AUGUSTINE ALPHA

*Published by Dorrance Publishing

For The Discerning Publishing
POB 45
Pontotoc, TX 76859
Visit our website at Amazon Author Central
ISBN: 9798842182305

Dedicated to: My husband, my work colleagues, and school colleague's, whom every one of them provided inspiration in some form.

Thank you for purchasing this book. You can't afford not to read it.

You will be taken on an adventure into a world few people have

the opportunity to experience. Some of the information in this book

is historical, some of it fictional.

World One Currency/World One Coin is a doctrine that has the

opportunity to change the world in a very significant way, those time

will be here sooner rather than later.

Introduction

Bank of England: "New forms of digital money would represent a different kind of innovation. This is both in the form of money offered and, in the infrastructure, used to make payments. Such innovation could boost economic activity. It could contribute to faster, cheaper, and more efficient payments with greater functionality. And it could open the door to future innovations that meet the evolving transaction needs of households and businesses. For example:

- New forms of digital money could enable cheaper payments through encouraging technological innovation and by increasing competition, lowering the costs faced by retailers when accepting payments.
- By offering real-time settlement, new forms of digital money could avoid the liquidity costs that are incurred by the multi-day settlement timeframe that currently often occurs. Monies exchanged would immediately belong to the recipient and the payment would be irrevocable (with refunds and returns processed as separate payments).
- As an independent means of payment, new forms of digital money could act as a contingency in the event of a disruption to other mechanisms. For example, they could help alleviate temporary problems with card payment networks.

- New forms of digital money could help meet future payment needs. For example, they could allow users to execute payments automatically based on some defined criteria – so called 'programmable money'. They might also enable payments for very small amounts – or 'micropayments' – if they allow small transactions to happen at a lower cost than today.
- New forms of digital money could further act as a potential building block towards better cross-border payments. This would mean, for example, that households and non-financial businesses could make cross-border payments quicker and cheaper. Importantly, however, this will also rely on other progress on, for instance, common settlement windows, compliance checks and messaging standards in different languages."

Chapter 1

World One Currency, World One Coin, WOC/C

World One Coin (WOCC)/Currency (WOC)

WOC Index would be a worldwide currency Index made up of all the currencies. The index is a value weighted index much like the NASDAQ. WOC is not meant to replace the individual country's Fiat currency. WOC is not controlled or influenced by a single Country (government). It is meant to provide stability and worldwide trade. It can be used internationally, domestically, commercially, retail and individual uses such as hedging, arbitrage, trading, investment and transactions. We will get it approved in every country and on every trading venue. Both WOC Fiat and WOCC token currency will be traded. Bitcoin has no fundamental basis to be used as a digital currency, WOC is based on the WOC Index. The WOC Index is all worldwide currencies/coin, weighted by volume divided by a divisible quotient, WOCC is the top 100 crypto coins weighted by volume divided by a divisible quotient.

Goals

- To allow anyone in the world access to sound money
- To preserve value
- To create tokens that are be convertible on demand to fiat or Crypto Currency.

- Open Source
- Could be used to create other commodity backed tokens
- Support for Fiat backed, and Crypto currency backed stable coins
- AML / KYC Compliant
- Trading, hedging, investment

Problems with Bitcoin, Ethereum and similar

cryptocurrencies:

- Unable to be used as unit of account and medium of exchange because of many factors including huge price swings. Stability of price is important when buying or selling goods or services and when sending or receiving payments.

World One Currency/Coin

WOC Foundation

World One Coin (WOCC)/Currency (WOC)Foundation

A healthy financial world. We use the best resources to provide the best recommendations.

The Foundation should be made up of Advisory Board members, Chairperson of the Board/CEO, President, and Committee Directors. The headquarters is in the most favorable Country/s. The Foundation provides the education and support for the WOCC/WOC Index and WOCC coin/WOC currency.

WOC currency will be in the following denominations:

.01 Of a WOC

.05 Of a WOC

.10 of a WOC

1 WOC

5 WOC

10 WOC

20 WOC

50 WOC

100 WOC

500 WOC

1000 WOC

Trading, hedging, Investment Opportunities

WOCC Index Coin

WOC Index Currency

WOCC Coin/Currency Pair

WOCC Coin/Bitcoin and all other crypto coins

WOC Currency/USD and all other currency's

Committees are;

WOC Government Committee

subcommittee; WOC G10

WOC G20

WOC G50

WOC Business Committee

subcommittee; WOC B 10

WOC B 20

WOC B 50

WOC Nonprofit Committee

Subcommittee; WOC NP-10

WOC NP20

WOC NP50

WOC Financial Institutions Committee

Subcommittee; WOC F 10

WOC F 20

WOC F 50

WOC Financial Education Committee

Individual

Organizations; For-Profit, Non-Profit

Schools

WOC Financial Crisis Committee

Government

Local

Regional

Country

- Business
  - Nationwide
  - Worldwide
- Financial Institution
  - Banking
  - Broker/Dealer
  - Money Management

WOC Event Committee

- Host Black-tie Event, raise money for local/Country/Worldwide Non-Profits and those businesses who work/support/partner with Non-Profits

WOC Financial IT Committee

- Cyber attacks
- Hackers
- AI

WOC Operations Committee

- HR
- Printing
- Facilities
- Finance/Accounting
- Legal
- Media

World One Currency/Coin (WOC)

The WOC Protocol: WOC

Abstract

The WOC Protocol, also known as the WOC (WOC) system, allows users to generate WOC assets approved by "WOC Governance." WOC Foundation Governance is the community organized and operated process of managing the various aspects of the WOC Protocol. WOC is a decentralized, unbiased, fiat and cryptocurrency pegged to the WOC Index. Resistant to hyperinflation due to its low volatility, WOC offers economic freedom and opportunity to anyone, anywhere.

This paper is a reader-friendly description of the Protocol, which is built on the blockchain. Technically savvy users might want to head directly to the introduction in the WOC Documentation for an in-depth explanation of the entire system.

About WOC is an open-source project on the blockchain and a Decentralized Autonomous Organization. The project is managed by people around the world who hold its governance token, WOCG. Through a system of governance involving Executive Voting and Governance Polling, WOCG holders manage the WOC Protocol and the financial risks of WOC to ensure its stability, transparency, and efficiency. WOCG voting weight is proportional to the amount of WOCG a voter stakes in the voting contract. In other words, the more WOCG tokens locked in the contract, the greater the voter's decision-making power.

About the WOC Protocol. The WOC Protocol, built on the blockchain, enables users to create currency. Current elements of the WOC Protocol are the WOC Foundation, WOC Oracles, and Voting. WOC governs the WOC Protocol by deciding on key parameters (e.g., fees, foundation direction, rates, etc.) through the voting power of WOCG holders.

The WOC Protocol, one of the largest decentralized applications (dapps) on the blockchain, will be the first decentralized finance (DeFi) application to earn significant adoption.

About the WOC Foundation, which is part of the global WOC community, will built and launched the WOC Protocol in conjunction with several outside partners. It is currently working with the community to bootstrap decentralized governance of the project and drive it toward complete decentralization.

About the WOC Foundation. The WOC Foundation, based in TBD, is self-governing and independent of the WOC Index. It was formed to house the WOC community's key intangible assets, such as trademarks and code copyrights, and it operates solely based on objective and rigid statutes that define its mandate. Its purpose, as noted in the Trust Deed, is to safeguard what cannot be technologically decentralized in the WOC Protocol.

Welcome to WOC (WOC)(WOCC).

In WOC We Trust

Blockchain technology provides an unprecedented opportunity to ease the public's growing frustration with—and distrust of—dysfunctional centralized financial systems. By distributing data across a network of computers, the technology allows any group of individuals to embrace transparency rather than central-entity control. The result is an unbiased, transparent, and highly efficient permissionless system—one that can improve current global financial and monetary structures and better serve the public good.

Bitcoin was created with this goal in mind. But, while Bitcoin succeeds as a cryptocurrency on several levels, it is not ideal as a medium of exchange because its fixed supply and speculative nature results in volatility, which prevents it from proliferating as mainstream money.

The WOC on the other hand, succeeds where Bitcoin fails precisely because WOC is designed to *minimize price volatility.* A decentralized, unbiased, Currency/cryptocurrency that is pegged to the WOC/C Index, WOC's value is in its stability.

Upon the release of WOC, it will become the building block for decentralized applications that help expand the DeFi (decentralized finance) movement. WOC's success is part of a wider industry movement designed to maintain price value and function like money.

For example, in February 2019, JPMorgan became the first bank in the United States to create and test a digital coin that represents 1 USD. As the cryptocurrency industry grows, other banks, financial services companies, and even governments will create stable digital currencies (e.g., Central Bank Digital Currencies), as will large organizations outside of the finance sector. Facebook, for example, announced its plans for Libra, “a stable digital cryptocurrency that will be fully backed by a reserve of real assets,” in June 2019. However, such proposals forfeit the core value proposition of blockchain technology: global adoption of a common infrastructure without a central authority or administrator that may abuse its influence.

An Overview of the WOC Protocol and Its Features

The WOC Protocol

The WOC Protocol will become one of the largest dapps on the blockchain. Designed by a disparate group of contributors, including developers within the WOC Foundation, its outside partners, and other persons and entities, it is the first decentralized finance (DeFi) application to see significant adoption.

The WOC Protocol is managed by people around the world who hold its governance token, WOCG. Through a system of governance involving Executive Voting and Governance Polling, WOCG holders govern the Protocol and the financial risks of WOC to ensure its stability, transparency, and efficiency. One WOCG token locked in a voting contract equals one vote.

The WOC

The WOC is a decentralized, unbiased, collateral-backed cryptocurrency soft-pegged to the US Dollar. WOC will be held within many platforms and will be supported on other popular exchanges.

WOC is easy to generate, access, and use. Users generate WOC by depositing into WOC accounts within the WOC Protocol. This is how WOC is entered into circulation and how users gain access to liquidity. Others obtain WOC by buying it from brokers or exchanges, or simply by receiving it as a means of payment.

Once generated, bought, or received, WOC can be used in the same manner as any other currency/cryptocurrency: it can be sent to others, used as payments for goods and services, and even held as savings.

Every WOC in circulation is directly priced by the WOC Index and all WOC transactions are publicly viewable on the blockchain.

WOC Index is a worldwide currency Index made up of all the currencies. The index is a value weighted index much like the NASDAQ. WOC is not meant to replace the individual country's Fiat currency. WOC is not controlled or influenced by a single Country (government). It is meant to provide stability and worldwide trade. It can be used internationally, domestically, commercially, retail, and individual uses such as hedging, arbitrage, trading, investment and transactions. We will get it approved in every country and on every trading venue. Both WOC Fiat and token currency will be traded. Bitcoin has no fundamental basis to be used as a digital currency, WOC is based on the WOC Index.

Generally, money has four functions:

1. A store of value
2. A medium of exchange
3. A unit of account
4. A standard of deferred payment

WOC has properties and use cases designed to serve these functions.

WOC as a Store of Value

A store of value is an asset that keeps its value without significant depreciation over time. Because WOC is based on a weight-index, it is designed to function as a store of value even in a volatile market.

WOC as a Medium of Exchange

A medium of exchange is anything that represents a standard of value and is used to facilitate the sale, purchase, or exchange (trade) of goods or services. The WOC will be used around the world for all types of transactional purposes.

WOC as a Unit of Account. A unit of account is a standardized measurement of value used to price goods and services (e.g., USD, EUR, YEN). Currently, WOC has a targeted price of all currencies, weighted by volume, indexed by a divisible divider. While WOC is not used as a standard measurement of value in the world, it functions as a unit of account within the WOC Protocol, whereby WOC Protocol accounting or pricing of services could be in WOC rather than a fiat currency like USD.

WOC as a Standard of Deferred Payment

WOC is used to settle debts within the WOC Protocol (e.g., users use WOC to pay the fee). This benefit separates WOC from other fees.

Collateral Assets

WOC is generated, backed, and kept stable through pricing of assets that are indexed in the WOC Protocol. The fiat asset or digital asset that WOCG holders are voted to accept into the Protocol.

To generate WOC, the WOC Protocol accepts any currency/coin-based asset that has been approved by WOCG holders. WOCG holders must also approve specific, corresponding Risk Parameters for each accepted asset (e.g., more stable assets might get more lenient Risk Parameters, while more risky assets could get stricter Risk Parameters). Detailed information on Risk Parameters is below. These and other decisions of WOCG holders are made through the WOC decentralized governance process.

WOC

All accepted assets can be leveraged to generate WOC in the WOC Protocol. Users can access the WOC Protocol and create WOC assets through several different user interfaces (i.e., network access portals). Creating a account/valet is not complicated, but generating WOC does create an obligation to pay the WOC Fee.

Users interact with WOC and the WOC Protocol directly, and each user has complete and independent control over their deposited asset.

Interacting with a WOC

- Step 1: Create and Collateralize a Vault or Account
  A user creates a Vault via the Oasis Borrow portal or a community-created interface, such as Instadapp, Zerion, or MyEtherWallet, by funding it with a specific type and amount of collateral that will be used to generate WOC. Once funded, a Vault is considered collateralized.
- Step 2: Generate WOC
  The owner initiates a transaction, and then confirms it to generate a specific amount of WOC in exchange for keeping her collateral locked in the Vault.
- Step 3: Pay the Fee
  To retrieve a portion or all of the collateral, a Vault owner must pay down or completely pay back the WOC she generated, plus the Fee. The Fee can be paid in WOC, Fiat or Coin.
- Step 4: Withdraw Collateral
  With the WOC returned and the Fee paid, the owner can withdraw all or some of her asset. Once all WOC is completely used and all the asset is empty until the owner chooses to make another deposit.

Liquidation of Risky WOC Vaults

To ensure there is always enough collateral in the WOC Protocol to cover the value of all outstanding debt (the amount of WOC outstanding valued at the Target Price), any WOC deemed too risky (according to parameters established by WOC Governance) is managed through automated WOC Protocol. The Protocol makes the determination after comparing the current price to the current WOC Index. Each currency/coin ratio is determined by WOCG voters based on the risk profile of the particular asset.

WOC Protocol

The WOC Protocol enables the system to maintain even price information. At the point of misalignment, the WOC Protocol takes collateral and subsequently sells it using an internal market-based auction mechanism. This is an Asset Auction.

The WOC received from the Auction is used to cover the WOC's outstanding obligations, including payment of the Penalty fee set by WOCG voters.

If enough WOC is bid in the Auction to fully cover the obligations plus the Liquidation Penalty, that auction converts to a Reverse Collateral Auction to sell as little collateral as possible. Any leftover collateral is returned to the original owner.

If the Auction does not raise enough WOC to cover the outstanding obligation, the deficit is converted into Protocol debt. Protocol debt is covered by the WOC in the WOC Buffer. If there is not enough WOC in the Buffer, the Protocol triggers a Debt Auction. During a Debt Auction, WOCG is minted by the system (increasing the amount of WOCG in circulation), and then sold to bidders for WOC.

WOC proceeds from the Collateral Auction go into the WOC Buffer, which serves as a buffer against an increase of WOCG overall supply that could result from future uncovered Collateral Auctions.

If WOC proceeds from auctions and Fee payments exceed the WOC Buffer limit (a number set by WOC Governance), they are sold through a Surplus Auction. During a Surplus Auction, bidders compete by bidding increasing amounts of WOCG to receive a fixed amount of WOC. Once the Surplus Auction has ended, the WOC Protocol autonomously destroys the WOCG collected, thereby reducing the total WOCG supply.

Example (Collateral Auction Process): A currency becomes underpriced due to market conditions. An Auction Keeper then detects the underpriced opportunity and initiates liquidation of the Vault, which kicks off a Collateral Auction.

Each auction has a bidding model to assist in winning auctions. A bidding model includes a price at which to bid for the asset. The Auction Keeper uses the price from its bidding model as the basis for its bids in the first phase of a Auction, where increasing WOC bids are placed for the set amount of the asset. This amount represents the price of the total WOC wanted from the collateral auction.

Now, let's say the Auction Keeper bids 5,000 WOC to meet this amount. The WOC bid is transferred from the Vault to the Collateral Auction contract. With enough WOC in the Collateral Auction contract to cover the system's debt plus the Liquidation Penalty, the first phase of the Collateral Auction is over.

To reach the price defined in its bidding model, the Auction Keeper submits a bid in the second phase of the Collateral Auction. In this phase, the objective is to return as much of the collateral to the owner as the market will allow. The bids that the Auction Keepers place are for fixed WOC amounts. For instance, the bidding model of the Keeper in this example seeks a bid price of 125 WOC, so it offers 5000 WOC. Additional WOC for this bid is transferred from the Vault Engine to the Collateral Auction. After the bid duration limit is reached and the bid expires, the Auction Keeper claims the winning bid and settles the completed Collateral Auction by collecting the won collateral.

Key External Actors.

In addition to its smart contract infrastructure, the WOC Protocol involves groups of external actors to maintain operations: Keepers, Oracles, and Global Settlers (Emergency Oracles), and WOC community members. Keepers take advantage of the economic incentives presented by the Protocol; Oracles and Global Settlers are external actors with special permissions in the system assigned to them by WOCG voters; and WOC community members are individuals and organizations that provide services.

Keepers

A Keeper is an independent (usually automated) actor that is incentivized by arbitrage opportunities to provide liquidity in various aspects of a decentralized system. In the WOC Protocol, market participants will sell WOC when the market price is above the Target Price and buy WOC when the market price is below the Target Price. Keepers participate in Surplus Auctions, Debt Auctions, and Collateral Auctions when WOC Vaults are liquidated.

Price Oracles

The WOC Protocol requires real-time information about the market price of the collateral assets in WOC to know when to trigger Liquidations.

The Protocol derives its internal collateral prices from a Oracle that consists of a broad set of individual nodes called Oracle Feeds. WOCG voters choose a set of trusted Feeds to deliver price information to the system through transactions. They also control how many Feeds are in the set.

To protect the system from an attacker attempting to gain control of most of the Oracles, the WOC Protocol receives price inputs through the (OSM), not from the Oracles directly. The OSM, which is a layer of defense between the Oracles and the Protocol, delays a price, allowing Emergency Oracles or a WOC Governance vote to freeze an Oracle if it is compromised. Decisions regarding Emergency Oracles and the price delay duration are made by WOCG holders.

Emergency Oracles

Emergency Oracles are selected by WOCG voters and act as a last line of defense against an attack on the governance process or on other Oracles. Emergency Oracles can freeze individual Oracles to mitigate the risk of many users trying to withdraw their assets from the WOC Protocol in a short period of time, as they have the authority to unilaterally trigger an Emergency Shutdown.

WOCG Teams

WOCG teams consist of individuals and service providers, who may be contracted through WOC Governance to provide specific services to WOCG. Members of WOCG teams are independent market actors and are not employed by the WOC Foundation.

The flexibility of WOC Governance allows the WOC community to adapt the WOCG team framework to suit the services needed by the ecosystem based on real-world performance and emerging challenges.

Examples of WOCG team member roles are the Governance Facilitator, who supports the communication infrastructure and processes of governance, and Risk Team members, who support WOC Governance with financial risk research and draft proposals for new regulations.

While the WOC Foundation has bootstrapped WOC Governance to date, it is anticipated that the WOCG will take full control, conduct WOCG votes, and fill these varied WOCG team roles soon.

Governance of the WOC Protocol

Use of the WOCG Token in WOC Governance

The WOCG token—the governance token of the WOC Protocol—allows those who hold it to *vote* on changes to the WOC Protocol. Note that anyone, not only WOCG holders, can *submit* proposals for an WOCG vote.

Any voter-approved modifications to the governance variables of the Protocol will likely not take effect immediately in the future; rather, they could be delayed by as much if voters choose to activate the Governance Security. The delay would give WOCG holders the opportunity to protect the system, if necessary, against a malicious governance proposal (e.g., a proposal that alters collateral parameters contrary to established monetary policies or that allows for security mechanisms to be disabled) by triggering a Shutdown.

Polling and Executive Voting

In practice, the WOC Governance process includes proposal polling and Executive Voting. Proposal polling is conducted to establish a rough consensus of community sentiment before any Executive Votes are cast. This helps to ensure that governance decisions are considered thoughtfully and reached by consensus prior to the voting process itself. Executive Voting is held to approve (or not) changes to the state of the system. An example of an Executive Vote could be a vote to ratify Risk Parameters for a newly accepted currency.

At a technical level, smart contracts manage each type of vote. A Proposal Contract is a smart contract with one or more valid governance actions programmed into it. It can only be executed once. When executed, it immediately applies its changes to the internal governance variables of the WOC Protocol. After execution, the Proposal Contract cannot be reused.

Any Ethereum/IP Address can deploy valid Proposal Contracts. WOCG token holders can then cast approval votes for the proposal that they want to elect as the Active Proposal. The address that has the highest number of approval votes is elected as the Active Proposal. The Active Proposal is empowered to gain administrative access to the internal governance variables of the WOC Protocol, and then modify them.

The WOCG Token's Role in Recapitalization

In addition to its role in WOC Governance, the WOC has a complementary role as the recapitalization resource of the WOC Protocol. If the system debt exceeds the surplus, the WOCG token supply may increase through a Debt Auction (see above) to recapitalize the system. This risk inclines WOCG holders to align and responsibly govern the WOC ecosystem to avoid excessive risk-taking.

WOCG Holder Responsibilities

WOCG holders can vote to do the following:

- Add a new asset(fiat/crypto) type with a unique set of Risk Parameters.
- Change the Risk Parameters of one or more existing asset types or add new Risk Parameters to one or more existing asset types.
- Modify the WOC/WOCC Index.
- Choose the set of Oracle Feeds.
- Choose the set of Emergency Oracles.
- Trigger Emergency Shutdown.
- Upgrade the system.

WOCG holders can also allocate funds from the WOC Buffer to pay for various infrastructure needs and services, including Oracle infrastructure and collateral risk management research. The funds in the WOC Buffer are revenues from Stability Fees, Liquidation Fees, and other income streams.

The governance mechanism of the WOC Protocol is designed to be as flexible as possible, and upgradeable. Should the system mature under the guidance of the community, more advanced forms of Proposal Contracts could, in theory, be used, including Proposal Contracts that are bundled. For example, one proposal contract may contain both an adjustment of a Stability Fee and Market Price. Nonetheless, those revisions will remain for WOCG holders to decide.

Risk Parameters Controlled by WOC Governance

Each WOC assets has its own unique set of Risk Parameters that enforce usage. The parameters are determined based on the risk profile and are directly controlled by WOCG holders through voting.

The Key Risk Parameters for WOC Vaults are:

- Debt Ceiling: A Debt Ceiling is the maximum amount of debt that can be created by a single asset type. WOC Governance assigns every asset type a Debt Ceiling, which is used to ensure sufficient diversification of the WOC Protocol collateral portfolio. Once a collateral type has reached its Debt Ceiling, it becomes impossible to create more debt unless some existing users pay back all or a portion of their debt.
- Stability Fee: The Stability Fee is an annual percentage yield calculated on top of how much WOC has been generated against a collateral. The fee is paid in WOC only, and then sent into the WOC Buffer.

- Liquidation Ratio: A low Liquidation Ratio means WOC Governance expects low price volatility of the collateral; a high Liquidation Ratio means high volatility is expected.
- Liquidation Penalty: The Liquidation Penalty is a fee added to a asset's total outstanding generated WOC when a Liquidation occurs. The Liquidation Penalty is used to encourage owners to keep appropriate asset levels.
- Collateral Auction Duration: The maximum duration of Collateral auctions is specific by WOCG. Debt and Surplus auction durations are global system parameters.
- Auction Bid Duration: Amount of time before an individual bid expires and closes the auction.
- Auction Step Size: This Risk Parameter exists to incentivize early bidders in auctions and prevent abuse by bidding a tiny amount above an existing bid.

Risk and Mitigation Responsibilities of Governance

The successful operation of the WOC Protocol depends on WOC Governance taking necessary steps to mitigate risks. Some of those risks are identified below, each followed by a mitigation plan.

A malicious attack on the smart contract infrastructure by a bad actor.

One of the greatest risks to the WOC Protocol is a malicious actor—a programmer, for example, who discovers a vulnerability in the contracts, and then uses it to break the Protocol or steal from it.

In the worst-case scenario, all decentralized digital assets held as collateral in the Protocol are stolen, and recovery is impossible.

Mitigation: The WOC Foundation's highest priority Protocol, and the strongest defense of the Protocol is Formal Verification. The WOC codebase will be the first codebase of a decentralized application to be verified.

In addition to formal system verification, security audits by the best security organizations in the industry, third-party (independent) audits, and bug bounties are part of roadmap. To review the formal verification report and various WOC Protocol audits, visit WOC's website/

These security measures provide a strong defense system; however, they are not infallible. Even with formal verification, the mathematical modeling of intended behaviors may be incorrect, or the assumptions behind the intended behavior itself may be incorrect.

A black swan events

A black swan event is a rare and critical surprise attack on a system. For the WOC Protocol, examples of a black swan event include:

- An attack on the collateral types that back WOC.
- A large, unexpected price decrease of one or more collateral types.

- A highly coordinated Oracle attack.
- A malicious WOC Governance proposal.

Please note that this list of potential "black swans" is not exhaustive and not intended to capture the extent of such possibilities.

Mitigation: While no one solution is failsafe, the careful design of the WOC Protocol (the Liquidation Ratio, Debt Ceilings, the Governance Security Module, the Oracle Security Module, Emergency Shutdown, etc.) in conjunction with good governance (e.g., swift reaction in a crisis, thoughtful risk parameters, etc.) help to prevent or mitigate potentially severe consequences of an attack.

Unforeseen pricing errors and market irrationality

Oracle price feed problems or irrational market dynamics that cause variations in the price of WOC for an extended period can occur. If confidence in the system is lost, rate adjustments or even WOCG dilution could reach extreme levels and still not bring enough liquidity and stability to the market.

Mitigation: WOC Governance incentivizes a sufficiently large capital pool to act as Keepers of the market to maximize rationality and market efficiency and allow the WOC supply to grow at a steady pace without major market shocks. As a last resort, Emergency Shutdown can be triggered to release collateral to WOC holders, with their WOC claims valued at the Target Price.

User Abandonment for Less Complicated Solutions

The WOC Protocol is a complex decentralized system. As a result of its complexity, there is a risk that inexperienced users will abandon the Protocol in favor of systems that may be easier to use and understand.

Mitigation: While WOC is easy to generate and use for most enthusiasts and the Keepers that use it for margin trading, newcomers might find the Protocol difficult to understand and navigate. Although WOC is designed in such a way that users need not comprehend the underlying mechanics of the WOC Protocol to benefit from it, the resources

consistently provided by the WOC community and the WOC Foundation help to ensure onboarding is as uncomplicated as possible.

The WOC Foundation

The WOC Foundation will play a role, along with independent actors, in maintaining the WOC Protocol and expanding its usage worldwide, while facilitating Governance. However, the WOC Foundation has no plans to dissolve once WOCG can manage Governance completely on its own. Should WOCG fail to sufficiently take the reins upon the WOC Foundation's dissolution, the future health of the WOC Protocol could be at risk.

Mitigation: WOCG holders are incentivized to prepare for the Foundation's Protocol. Moreover, successful management of the system should result in sufficient funds for governance to allocate to the continued maintenance and improvement of the WOC Protocol.

General Issues with Experimental Technology

Users of the WOC Protocol (including but not limited to WOC and WOCG holders) understand and accept that the software, technology, and technical concepts and theories applicable to the WOC Protocol are still unproven and there is no warranty that the technology will be uninterrupted or error-free. There is an inherent risk that the technology could contain weaknesses, vulnerabilities, or bugs causing, among other things, the complete failure of the WOC Protocol and/or its component parts.

Mitigation: See “A malicious attack on the infrastructure by a bad actor” above. The Mitigation section there explains the technical auditing in place to ensure the WOC Protocol functions as intended.

Price Stability Mechanisms

The WOC Target Price

The WOC Target Price is used to determine the value of collateral assets WOC holders receive. The Target Price for WOC is the WOC Index.

Emergency Shutdown

Emergency Shutdown (or, simply, Shutdown) serves two main purposes. First, it is used during emergencies as a last-resort mechanism to protect the WOC Protocol against attacks on its infrastructure and directly enforce the WOC Target Price. Emergencies could include malicious governance actions, hacking, security breaches, and long-term market irrationality. Second, Shutdown is used to facilitate a WOC Protocol system upgrade. The Shutdown process can only be controlled by WOC Governance.

WOCG voters are also able to instantly trigger an Emergency Shutdown by depositing WOCG into the Emergency Shutdown Module (ESM), if enough WOCG voters believe it is necessary. This prevents the Governance Security Module (if active) from delaying Shutdown proposals before they are executed. With Emergency Shutdown, the moment a quorum is reached, the Shutdown takes effect with no delay.

There are three phases of Emergency Shutdown:

1. The WOC Protocol shuts down; owners withdraw assets.
   When initiated, Shutdown prevents further creation and manipulation of existing assets, and freezes the Price Feeds. The frozen feeds ensure that all users are able to withdraw the net value of assets to which they are entitled. Effectively, it allows WOC owners to immediately withdraw the collateral in their account that is not actively backing a transaction.
2. Post-Emergency Shutdown auction processing

After Shutdown is triggered, Collateral Auctions begin and must be completed within a specific amount of time. That time period is determined by WOC Governance to be slightly longer than the duration of the longest Collateral Auction. This guarantees that no auctions are outstanding at the end of the auction processing period.

3. WOC holders claim their remaining collateral.

At the end of the auction processing period, WOC holders use their WOC to claim collateral directly at a fixed rate that corresponds to the calculated value of their assets based on the WOC Target Price. The user will be able to claim from the WOC Protocol after the auction processing period. There is no time limit for when a final claim can be made. WOC holders will get a proportional claim to each collateral type that exists in the collateral portfolio. Note that WOC holders could be at risk of a haircut, whereby they do not receive the full value of their WOC holdings at the Target Price. This is due to risks related to declines in collateral value and to owners having the right to retrieve their excess before WOC holders may claim the remaining collateral. For more detailed information on Emergency Shutdown, including the claim priorities that would occur as a result.

The Future of the WOC Protocol: Increased Adoption and Full Decentralization

Addressable Market

A currency with price stability serves as an important medium of exchange for many decentralized applications. As such, the potential market for WOC is at least as large as the entire decentralized industry. But the promise of WOC extends well beyond that into other industries.

The following is a non-exhaustive list of current and immediate markets for the WOC:

- Working capital, hedging, and collateralized leverage. WOC allows for permissionless trading by users, who can use the WOC against asset collateral for working capital. There will be numerous instances where owners use their WOC to buy additional assets (same asset as their collateral), thereby creating a leveraged but fully collateralized position.
- Merchant receipts, cross-border transactions, and remittances. Foreign exchange volatility mitigation and a lack of intermediaries mean the transaction costs of international trade are significantly reduced when using WOC.
- Charities and NGOs when using transparent distributed ledger technology.
- Gaming. For blockchain game developers, WOC will be the currency of choice. With WOC, game developers integrate not only a currency, but also an entire economy. The composability of WOC allows games to create new player behavior schemes based around decentralized finance.

- Prediction markets. Using a volatile crypto/currency when making an unrelated prediction only increases one's risk when placing the bet. Long-term bets become especially infeasible if the bettor must also gamble on the future price of the volatile asset used to place the bet. That said, the WOC would be a natural choice for use in prediction markets.

- Trading, hedging, Investment Opportunities
    - WOCC Index Coin
    - WOC Index Currency
    - WOCC Coin/Currency Pair
    - WOCC Coin/Bitcoin and all other crypto coins
    - WOC Currency/USD and all other currency's

Asset Expansion

Should WOCG holders approve new assets as collateral, those assets will be subject to the same risk requirements, parameters, and safety measures as WOC (e.g., Liquidation Ratios, Stability Fees, Savings Rates, Debt Ceilings, etc.).

Evolving Oracles. WOCG will be the first project to run reliable Oracles. As a result, many decentralized applications use WOCG Oracles to ensure the security of their systems and to provide up-to-date price data in a robust manner. This confidence in WOCG and the WOC Protocol means that WOC Governance can expand the core Oracle infrastructure service to better suit the needs of decentralized applications.

Chapter 2

WOC

The WOC Protocol allows users to generate WOC, a stable store of value that lives entirely on the currency/coin markets. WOC is a decentralized Index that is not issued or administered by any centralized actor or trusted intermediary or counterparty. It is unbiased and borderless —available to anyone, anywhere.

Anyone with an internet connection can monitor the health of the system anytime.

With hundreds of partnerships and one of the strongest developer communities in the market, WOCG will be become the engine of the decentralized finance (DeFi) movement. WOC is unlocking the power of the market to deliver on the promise of economic empowerment today.

WOC Use-Case Benefits and Examples

The WOC Protocol can be used by anyone, anywhere, without any restrictions or personal-information requirements. Below are a few examples of how WOC can be used around the world:

WOC Offers Financial Independence to All

According to the World Bank's Global Findex Database 2017, about 1.7 billion adults around the world are unbanked. In the US alone, according to a 2017 survey by the FDIC, around 32 million American households are either unbanked or underbanked, meaning that they either have no bank account at all or they regularly use alternatives to traditional banking (e.g., payday or pawn shop loans) to manage their finances. WOC can empower every one of those people; all they need is access to the internet.

As the world's first unbiased Currency/Coin, WOC allows anyone to achieve financial independence, regardless of their location or circumstances. For example, in Latin America, WOC can provided an opportunity for individuals and families to hedge against the devaluation of the Argentine peso and the Venezuelan Bolívar.

Self-Sovereign Money Generation

Oasis Borrow allows users to access the WOC Protocol and generate WOC by locking their collateral in a WOC. Notably, users do not need to access any third-party intermediary to generate WOC. Vaults/accounts offer individuals and businesses opportunities to create liquidity on their assets simply, quickly, and at relatively low cost.

Bank of England: "New forms of digital money would represent a different kind of innovation. This is both in the form of money offered and, in the infrastructure, used to make payments. Such innovation could boost economic activity. It could contribute to faster, cheaper, and more efficient payments with greater functionality. And it could open the door to future innovations that meet the evolving transaction needs of households and businesses. For example:

- New forms of digital money could enable cheaper payments through encouraging technological innovation and by increasing competition, lowering the costs faced by retailers when accepting payments.
- By offering real-time settlement, new forms of digital money could avoid the liquidity costs that are incurred by the multi-day settlement timeframe that currently often occurs. Monies exchanged would immediately belong to the recipient and the payment would be irrevocable (with refunds and returns processed as separate payments).
- As an independent means of payment, new forms of digital money could act as a contingency in the event of a disruption to other mechanisms. For example, they could help alleviate temporary problems with card payment networks.
- New forms of digital money could help meet future payment needs. For example, they could allow users to execute payments automatically based on some defined criteria – so called 'programmable money'. They might also enable payments for very small amounts – or 'micropayments' – if they allow small transactions to happen at a lower cost than today.

- New forms of digital money could further act as a potential building block towards better cross-border payments. This would mean, for example, that households and non-financial businesses could make cross-border payments quicker and cheaper. Importantly, however, this will also rely on other progress on, for instance, common settlement windows, compliance checks and messaging standards in different languages."

Chapter 3

Countries that went bankrupt.

1. Greece

Location: Europe

Date: 2015

Currency: Euro

GDP in 2019: 326 billion dollars

Population: 10.7 million

Greece is a European country which was not among the most developed countries in Europe until they've joined the European Union in 1981. As a member of the EU, their economy has started strengthening, but that was not enough to avoid bankruptcy in 2015. There were a few things that led to the bankruptcy of this country.

First of all, the Greek economy was affected by the Great Recession. This recession had an impact on a few western countries too, but it was felt the most by Greece and it became one of the rare developed countries that went bankrupt in the last 50 years. In addition to the external factors, there were a few internal factors that contributed to the bankruptcy including poor GDP growth, budget compliance, government debt, and continuous deficits and data credibility.

With the help of European banks, Greece managed to cover part of the debt and get out of bankruptcy after a short period of time. When it comes to the economy of this country which is part of the Eurozone, tourism, agriculture pharmaceuticals are some of the main industries that drive their economy.

- One of the rare European countries that went bankrupt in the last 50 years
- They managed to cover the debt in less than 3 weeks with the help of their European partners
- Greece is part of Eurozone

2. Russia

Location: Europe/Asia

Date: 1918

Currency: Ruble

GDP in 2019: 4.36 trillion dollars

Population: 146 million

Back in 1918, Russia was known as the Russian Soviet Federative Socialist Republic, a predecessor of the Soviet Union. These were hard times for Russia and the rest of republics which part of this socialist state. The wounds of the civil war at home and the effects of World War I have devastated their economy.

After the October Revolution, Russia was forced to go bankrupt because the leader of the newly formed socialist state – Lenin – refused to pay the debts created by the Russian tsars which were expelled to the Western countries after the revolution. So, this is one of the countries that went bankrupt which created a more negative impact on the residents of other countries than to itself.

Since most of the guarantors of Russian debts were located in France, the nationals of this country were the most affected people by this bankruptcy. After the dissolution of the Soviet Union in 1991, Russia agreed to pay these debts. Nowadays, Russia is becoming a big player in the global market which means that it's possible to recover and re-establish a good position after bankruptcy. One of the most important factors that have contributed to this recovery is the presence of natural resources in Russia.

- Russia was known as the Russian Soviet Federative Socialist Republic in 1918 when the bankruptcy happened
- This is one of the countries that went bankrupt that refused to pay debts to foreign financial institutions.
- The debt was cleared about 70 years later

3. Iceland

Location: Europe

Date: 2008

Currency: Krona

GDP in 2019: 19 billion dollars

Population: 358.000

Before this country went bankrupt, it was known as an economical wonder for a few years. People from all over the world were going to this isolated island located in northwest Europe in order to work there because this country had an excellent standard and quality of life.

However, in 2008, Iceland joined the countries that went bankrupt when three of the most used privately-owned banks in Iceland were forced to stop their operations. As a result of that, Iceland went into political unrest, but things have started going in the right direction in 2011. According to many experts, the main reason why Iceland went bankrupt was the fact that they have given too much power to the private commercial banks back in 2001.

- Iceland is one of the countries that went bankrupt in the 21st century
- The main cause was the poor financial planning of the main banks of this country
- The crisis stopped after three years in 2011

4. Germany

Location: Europe

Date: 1923

Currency: Deutsche Mark

GDP in 2019: 4.5 trillion dollars

Population: 82 million

Germany is one of the leaders of the global economy today. But, it wasn't always like this. Back in the 1920s, Germany was trying to recover from World War I losses. They had to pay their debts to the victorious sides in this war, but they simply couldn't find the money.

One bread was worth 200 billion Deutsch marks which is obviously a great sign about the extent of the inflation in this country. In 1923, German people were forced to bring bags with them to the grocery stores in order to put the money they needed to buy food. The value of the Deutsch mark was dropping every minute.

The extreme debts and the consequences of World War I have led to this incredible hyperinflation. This was an unpleasant burden that a few other generations of Germans had to carry with them. Most historians agree that the bankruptcy in 1923 had contributed to the rise of the Nazi ideology and the cult of Adolf Hitler.

- The hyperinflation that you cannot find in another country

- Germany was one of the countries that went bankrupt due to its military loss in the WWI
- One of the causes of World War II

5. Mexico

Location: North America

Date: 1994

Currency: Peso

GDP in 2019: 2.6 trillion dollars

Population: 126.5 million

Let's be clear, Mexico has never been a financial giant in the region, but they definitely had better times than what the nation has witnessed in 1994. Before we go into details, let us say that today Mexico is facing problems with emigration. Many of their residents are looking for a way to emigrate to the United States, both legally and illegally. Both qualified and unqualified workers are trying to get to the US where they can earn more money.

In 1994, Mexico made it to the list of countries that went bankrupt at least for a short period of time. This debt crisis is known as the Mexican peso crisis. Obviously, this was a currency crisis which came as a result of the fast devaluation of Mexico's national currency – the peso – against the US dollar.

Capital flight was the main reason behind this problem which threatened to ruin Mexico's economy. In the background, it was the political instability which made investors boost risk premium on Mexican assets. The US Congress had to pass the Mexican Debt Disclosure Act in order to solve this problem. Of course, the effects of this crisis were felt in Mexico for a long period of time.

- Mexico is a country which has many ups and downs when it comes to the national economy
- This is one of the countries that went bankrupt and were bailed out with the help of the US
- This part of Mexico's financial history is known as the Peso crisis

6. Denmark

Location: Europe

Date: 1813

Currency: Krone

GDP in 2019: 300 billion dollars

Population: 5.8 million

Denmark is a Nordic country which is present on many lists of countries with the highest quality of living, highest incomes and other lists that can confirm that this country has a strong economy. However, there were times in the past when the Danish economy was struggling. For instance, back in 1813, Denmark became one of the few countries that went bankrupt.

All the countries that went bankrupt back then were affected by the Napoleonic Wars. Denmark has participated in these wars and they had to issue more banknotes than they could afford to issue which made their monetary system quite weak. Even though Denmark was trying to remain neutral, England had its doubts and occupied parts of Denmark which sped up the bankruptcy.

- One of the countries that went bankrupt due to the Napoleonic Wars
- Denmark is one of the most developed countries in the world today
- They wanted to stay neutral in the Napoleonic Wars, but other countries had their doubts about their neutrality

7. Argentina

Location: South America

Date: 2001

Currency: Peso

GDP in 2019: 920 billion dollars

Population: 43.8 million

The 1990s were one of the golden eras of the Argentinian economy. They were basically the leaders of South American countries at this time and their economy was looking very promising. However, the authorities of this country have made a few mistakes that led to one of the worst financial crisis in this country.

In 2001, Argentina owed over 100 billion dollars to domestic and international entities. The unemployment rate has reached 20%. As a result of that, the political situation became very unstable and the country went bankrupt. Some of the reasons why there was a crisis is the fact that the peso was pegged to the US dollar, the public debt was not managed well and the corruption was thriving.

The good thing is that Argentina managed to stabilize its economy and the economy of this country looks good today. We should also mention that the crisis in 2001 was not the first time Argentina faced bankruptcy.

- Argentina went bankrupt in 2001
- Corruption and poor public debt management were some of the reasons that led to bankruptcy
- Today, Argentina has a stable economy

8. Thailand

Location: Asia

Date: 1997

Currency: Baht

GDP in 2019: 1.4 trillion dollars

Population: 68.8 million

Similar to other countries on this list, Thailand was actually doing great before a financial crisis hit this country in Southeast Asia. Before they went bankrupt in 1997, their economy was growing and expanding at an excellent rate in the past ten years. The inflation rate was acceptable too. They have pegged their national currency (the baht) at 25 to the US dollar.

It was the series of speculative attacks that forced the government of Thailand to break the bond between the Baht and the US dollar and allowed the value to be dictated by the currency market. This has caused a domino effect which has hit the economy in a negative way.

Thailand was forced to go bankrupt and ask for help from the International Monetary Fund. The good thing is that it took just four years for the economy of this country to get back on track. They've paid their debts before the deadline allowing their economy to grow again.

- Thailand went bankrupt in 1997
- This event led to a financial crisis in a few other Asian countries
- The recovery of the national economy of this country was fast and smooth

9. Barbados

Location: North America

Date: 2018

Currency: Barbadian dollar

GDP in 2019: 7 billion dollars

Population: 277.000

Barbados has become an independent country in 1966. After the initial success in the field of economy in the first two decades, the island nation has started experiencing problems. Just like many other countries in this region, they couldn't rely only on tourism as an industry that will drive the economy. This country has tried attracting foreign investors by providing good offshore investment opportunities.

In the last 20 years, the economy of this country is experiencing many problems. In 2018, these problems have reached their climax when the government of Barbados informed the citizens that their country went bankrupt. They have revealed that they are defaulting their bonds due to the enormous debt.

They had a debt worth 7.5 billion dollars which is very high when we compare it to their GDP. The authorities are still looking for a permanent solution to this problem, but until then they are taking short-term measures that can help them avoid even more complicated situations for their economy.

- An island nation located in the Caribbean
- Barbados is one of the countries with the worst debt-to-GDP ratio in the world
- They went bankrupt in 2018

10. Venezuela

Location: South America

Date: 2017

Currency: Petro Bolivar Soberano

GDP in 2019: 76 billion dollars

Population: 31.5 million

Venezuela is one of the largest countries in South America. This is also one of the countries that have won their independence at the beginning of the 19th century thanks to leaders like Simon Bolivar. However, in the past couple of decades, Venezuela is experiencing political turmoil at home.
Before we go into details, let us say that the economy of this country relies primarily on the petroleum industry and manufacturing.

This is one of the places which have the richest sources of oil. Yet, for many reasons, Venezuela has been on a brink of a total economic collapse since 2015. One of the reasons for that is the presidency of Hugo Chavez and Nicolas Maduro. These Venezuelan leaders had strong disagreements with the leaders of the Western countries which made many of these countries to impose sanctions. In 2017, Venezuela went bankrupt.

They simply didn't have enough money to pay their lenders. This was one of the effects of the sanctions imposed by the United States in 2017. Today, Venezuela is on a brink of civil war and the opposition leaders are throwing rallies and protests all the time making it hard for the government to establish control and consolidate the economy of this country.

- The financial crisis started in 2015
- Venezuela went bankrupt in 2017
- Venezuela is one of the biggest oil exporters in the world

11. The United States of America

Location: North America

Date: 1840

Currency: US dollar

GDP in 2019: 20.8 trillion dollars

Population:327 million

The United States of America might be the country with the most powerful economy today, but it wasn't always like that. There were actually a few times when this country went bankrupt. One of these cases was the country default in 1840. Following the Panic of 1837, an event that has shaken the economy of the US, 19 out of 26 states that were part of the United States went bankrupt in the early 1840s.

What makes this case interesting is the direct cause of this problem. Namely, according to many experts, it was canal building that led to this issue. The country was focused on canal building and this activity required money. The national debt has reached 80 million dollars in just a few years. The infrastructure projects were booming across the states and new banks were looking for capital.

It's worth mentioning that creditors could not use military assistance to pay these debts because they had to fight states in order to do this. But, it turned out that the investment projects that were taken by these states were worth it. It didn't take more than a few years for these states to pay their debts. Needless to say, these projects contributed to the development of the United States in general.

- More than half of the US states at that time went bankrupt
- They were investing in infrastructure projects more than they could afford
- The debts were paid off after a short period of time

12. Newfoundland

Location: North America

Date: 1933

Currency: Canadian dollar

GDP in 2019: 1.9 trillion dollars (Canada)

Population: 37.3 million (Canada)

Did you know that Newfoundland was once a sovereign state? It was part of the British Dominion, but the territory was self-governing. This means that the local authorities had the freedom to pass laws and bills and to manage their economy in any way they want. However, it turns out that they didn't know how to run the economy in the right way.

Starting from the late 19th century, the authorities have invested a lot in railway construction. They have also created their own regiment which was part of the First World War. All these things made sense at the time, but they also cost a lot of money. The debts have started mounting and the British government has created a special Royal Commission focused on Newfoundland's economy.

As a result of that, they have lost their self-governing status. Newfoundland was managed by a commissioner appointed by the UK. In 1949, Newfoundland became part of Canada, it's the tenth province to be more precise.

- Newfoundland was a self-governing region at the beginning of the 20th century
- It later becomes part of the UK with no self-governing privileges
- The huge investment in infrastructural projects led to bankruptcy

13. Belize

Location: North America

Date: 2012

Currency: Belizean dollar

GDP in 2019: 3.3 billion dollars

Population: 398.000

Belize is a small independent country located in Central America. It has a population of just 388.000. Belize, like other countries in this region, has a private enterprise economy which is focused on agriculture and merchandising. Tourism and construction are two of the most important industries here. For many years, Belize was known as a tax haven where thousands of international offshore companies are registered.

However, this small country has struggled with its economy for many years. Poor tax collection, lack of basic natural resources and other factors contributed to the growing debt of this country. Back in 2012, Belize missed 23 million interest payment.

This amount of money might seem like a small debt for many people, but it was enough to hurt Belize's economy and force the government to declare bankruptcy at least for a short period of time. With debt restructuring and negotiations with debt collectors, this country managed to end this financial crisis.

- Belize is located in Central America
- It went bankrupt in 2012
- This country is known as a tax haven

14. Zimbabwe

Location: Africa

Date: 2007

Currency: RTGS dollar and US dollar

GDP in 2019: 41billion dollars

Population: 16.1 million

Zimbabwe was one of the few countries in Africa that were still not independent in the late 1970s. They gained their independence in 1980. In the first years of their independence, the country has witnessed excellent growth and strengthening of the economy.

However, starting from 1991, Robert Mugabe, the president of Zimbabwe has introduced an Economic Structural Adjustment Program which had a negative impact on the economy of this African country. This program was targeting British farmers and this led to problems with the international community. The direct result of that was famine, decreased life expectancy, and continuous financial crisis.

In 2007, Zimbabwe went bankrupt and the world has witnessed another hyperinflation. According to some statistics, inflation reached an incredible 89.7 sextillion percent in 2008. The government was forced to drop their currency which was replaced with fiat currencies of other nations primarily US dollars. This currency change has helped Zimbabwe to get out of the risk zone, but the economic instability of this country is still in place. It will take serious reforms and better budgeting in order to resolve this situation.

- Zimbabwe became an independent country in 1980
- The financial crisis in this country started in 1991 and culminated in 2007
- Zimbabwe uses the US dollar as official currency

15. The United Kingdom

Location: Europe

Date: 1976

Currency: Pound sterling

GDP in 2019: 3 trillion dollars

Population: 66.9 million

The United Kingdom is currently stuck in the Brexit process which should help this country leave the European Union. It turned out that the people of this country were interested in managing their funds in their own way. Historically, they have a good record when it comes to this activity and the UK has always had a strong economy.

However, there were times when things were not going as planned and the UK had to look for radical solutions. We are not sure whether we can say that the United Kingdom went bankrupt in 1976, but this was a year when the British needed international help to support economic stability in their country.

So, in 1976, the British government had to borrow around 4 billion dollars from the IMF (International Monetary Fund). This was the highest loan that was requested until then. After getting around 50% of the loan and making serious budget cuts, the government was able to stabilize the economy of the country. The loan was later repaid, but for a few years, the UK had to follow the instructions provided by the IMF.

- The United Kingdom was facing a serious financial crisis in 1976
- The IMF helped the UK avoid complete bankruptcy
- This was one of the highest loans of all time approved by the IMF

16. Bolivia

Location: South America

Date: 1984

Currency: Boliviano

GDP in 2019: 95 billion dollars

Population: 11.4 million

Bolivia is one of the two landlocked countries located in South America. This country has been independent for over 150 years now and just like the rest of the countries in this region, it had its ups and downs. The same goes for the economy of this country.

The best period for the Bolivian economy was between 1960 and 1977. A fee of the most important sectors of the national economy of this country was growing fast like the agricultural sector and the mining industry. However, things started going wrong after that. It was the fixed exchange rate policy which was followed without any modifications for many years and the continuous deficits that resulted in a debt crisis which started in 1978 and culminated in 1984 when the entire continent witnessed a financial crisis.

All the hard work in the field of the economy was lost in just a few years. Bolivia went bankrupt in 1984 when the inflation rate reached over 20.000%. The good thing is that the government has introduced radical measures in the monetary sector and the fiscal sector which stabilized the inflation rate and economy in general. It's good to know that Bolivia had a financial crisis at the beginning of the 2010s too.

- Bolivia is a country with an economy that primarily relies on agriculture and mining
- They went bankrupt in 1984

- The main import and export partner of Bolivia is Brazil

17. Yugoslavia

Location: Europe

Date: 1982

Currency: Dinar

GDP in 2019: –

Population: 22.5 million (in 1981)

This is an example of a country that went bankrupt which no longer exists. Yugoslavia was a socialist state which existed in Southeast Europe between 1945 and 1992. Six independent states were created as a result of the disintegration of this country.

In 1982, Yugoslavia went bankrupt, but the socialist regime managed to hide this fact. So, this might not have been a de jure bankruptcy, but it was definitely a de facto bankruptcy. In this year, Yugoslavia failed to find funds to take care of foreign loans. The consequences for the economy of this country were felt everywhere – limits on funds that you can transport across the border, lack of foreign goods and an agreement with the IMF about loans and financial support. The debt was reallocated to the republics which part of the federative state. These debts were being paid for many years after the disintegration of the country.

- Yugoslavia is a former country which was located in Southeast Europe

- It included six republics which later became independent countries
- This county went bankrupt in 1982

Chapter 4

Changing World Order

The Raise and Fall of the Great Powers, this is happening while the World is collapsing. Ray Diablo in his book "Changes in the World Order" and Paul Kennedy in his book "The Raise and Fall or the Great Powers" clearly outlined the key indicators and the expected results for the world, countries, corporations and the people within it.

This should come as no surprise. If you're trusted with investment money you are doing a disservice if you are "not a student of financial history".

Ray Diablo: EXPANDED ANALYSIS OF THE CONDITIONS OF, AND PROSPECTS FOR, THE

WORLD'S LEADING COUNTRIES

As he described in his book *Principles for Dealing with the Changing World Order*, he automated the way of looking at the cause/effect relationships that are driving both improvements in and worsening of countries' conditions so that data is fed into a computer that analyzes it and writes a summary of the current conditions and the long-term prospects for each country. This is done for the world's 24 leading countries.

Ray "To understand how it works and how I use it, imagine you are a chess player and that you built a computerized version of your thinking process that analyzes and makes moves next to you while you also think through the moves you'd make. While it reflects your thinking, has perfect memory, and can process vast amounts of data almost instantaneously, the computer has no common sense and isn't able to pick up on subtle, non-quantifiable relationships. Your mind and the computer each bring different strengths and weaknesses that make you together far better than either of you alone. That's what it's like.

In my book I showed the computerized assessment of 11 major powers and promised to share updated versions for 24 countries—those in the G20 plus others that scored as notable global powers—at least annually on economicprinciples.org. That's what I'm now doing.

In this memo, I start by showing summary tables of scores of the 18 major determinants across countries (see *Principles for Dealing with the Changing World Order* for more details). After that, I show the computer-generated summaries that describe each country. The text for each country highlights a few of the major gauges and a few of the stats within each gauge that reflect the broad trends I am seeing. Of course, there is a great deal more below these summaries that I can delve into, though these summaries are good enough for our purposes.

The overall country power score is created by weighing the outputs of the 18 gauges, each of which is derived as a composite of several stats we aggregate based on relevance, quality, and consistency across countries and time. Because both the size of a country and the strength of the powers matter, I show measures of the total power and the per capita power of each country. For more detail on how I these about different types of measures (in per capita and absolute terms), please see the table at the end of this report, following the computer-generated country summaries.

To be clear, while these indices aren't perfect because the data through time isn't perfect and not everything can be captured in the data, they do an excellent job of painting the big picture. Additionally, it is worth noting that we have updated and improved the analysis since the book was published, which is why you may notice some figures differ slightly in this report compared to the publication. This system is a never-ending work in progress so you should expect it to evolve and continuously get better. I hope that you will find it as helpful as I find it. I also hope that these objective measures will lead to people objectively assessing policy makers' moves and that that will lead either to better policies or to better policy makers who will make better policies.

[As of April 2022]"

	GAUGE QUALITY	USA		CHN		EUR		DEU		JPN		KOR	
EMPIRE SCORE (0–1)		0.89		0.76	▲	0.58		0.38		0.33	▼	0.31	
THE BIG CYCLES													
Economic/Financial Position	Reliable	-1.5	▼	0.3	▼	-0.9		-0.1		-1.3		0.1	
Debt Burden (Big Economic Cycle)	Reliable	-1.9		0.0	▼	-0.6		0.8	▲	-1.0		0.5	
Expected Growth (Big Economic Cycle)	Reliable	-0.6		0.4	▼	-1.0		-1.0		-1.1		-0.4	▼
Internal Order	So-So	-2.0	▼	0.2		0.2	▲	0.8		1.1	▲	...	...
Gaps in Wealth, Opportunity & Values	So-So	-1.8	▼	0.2		0.1	▲	0.8		1.0	▲	0.0	
Internal Conflict[1] (Internal Order; low is bad)	Reliable	-2.2	▼	0.1		0.3		0.7		1.2	▲	...	...
External Order[2]	So-So	-1.3	▼	-1.3	▼	0.3		0.3		0.4		...	...
KEY EIGHT MEASURES OF POWER													
Education	Reliable	2.0		1.7	▲	0.4		-0.2		0.1		0.1	
Innovation & Technology	Reliable	2.1		1.6	▲	0.2		-0.2		0.1		0.2	
Cost Competitiveness	Reliable	-0.4		1.1		-0.6		-0.6		-0.3		0.1	
Military Strength	Reliable	2.0		0.9	▲	0.4		-0.7		-0.4		-0.4	
Trade	Reliable	1.1		1.9	▲	1.3		0.5		-0.5	▼	-0.7	
Economic Output	Reliable	1.7		1.5	▲	1.0	▼	-0.1		-0.1	▼	-0.9	▲
Markets & Financial Center	Reliable	2.7		0.2	▲	0.4		-0.2		0.1		-0.6	
Reserve Currency Status[3]	Reliable	1.9		-0.6		0.3		...	...	-0.5		-0.7	...
ADDITIONAL MEASURES OF POWER													
Geology	Reliable	1.6		0.5		-0.6		-0.7		-1.0		-0.9	
Resource-Allocation Efficiency	So-So	1.4		0.8		-0.8		1.0	▲	0.6		-0.5	▼
Acts of Nature	So-So	-0.2	...	-0.1	...	0.1	...	1.1	...	1.5	...	1.6	...
Infrastructure & Investment	Reliable	0.7		2.6	▲	0.4		-0.3		-0.2	▼	0.0	
Character/Civility/Determination	So-So	1.0		1.6		-1.0		-0.4		0.4		1.0	▼
Governance/Rule of Law	Reliable	0.7		-0.6		-0.5	...	0.7		0.8		-0.2	

Final note

Having a global currency can benefit everyone in some ways. There would be no currency risk in international trades and no fear of currency fluctuations for cross-border traders. Besides, it can omit the international transaction fees. Nowadays, cryptocurrencies are literally making this possible by presenting themselves as a secure, straightforward, and quick mode of financial transactions. Lastly, the concept of global currency is inevitable; therefore, it is better to embrace it with an open arm and appreciate the convenience.

Reference: The Economist

About the Author

Dr. Michelle Augustine, a passionate and open-minded individual who is supported by years of experience. Drawing on more than forty years of experience as Bond Trader, Hedge Fund Trader, Broker/Dealer Owner, CFO for a $10.5 billion pension system, and Chairperson for The College for Financial Planning.

Dr. Augustine looks for every opportunity to further the investment communities' knowledge and understanding of Investment Portfolio Management while establishing meaningful connection with clients.

Dr. Michelle P. Augustine shares very useful information regarding the world of finance.

Dr. Augustine shares the strategy behind this valuable information, helping those who are interested in joining the world of investment.

Dr. Augustine also shares what the world financially may look like in the future based on history.

Dr. Augustine holds a Ph.D. in Finance at Nova Southeastern University.

WORLD ONE CURRENCY

For The Discerning Publishing

PO Box 45

Pontotoc, TX 76869

ForTheDiscerningPublishing.com

FTDPublishing.com

DrMichelleAugustine.com

ISBN:9798842182305

www.ingramcontent.com/pod-product-compliance
Lightning Source LLC
LaVergne TN
LVHW090133160826
845673LV00017B/2454

* 9 7 9 8 8 4 2 1 8 2 3 0 5 *